How to Prune
FRUIT TREES

HOW TO PRUNE FRUIT TREES

R. SANFORD MARTIN

With Excerpts from
H. H. Thomas's *Pruning Made Easy*

EDITED BY CHRISTINE SCHULTZ

ECHO POINT BOOKS & MEDIA, LLC

Contents

•

Contents

●

———— ● ————

EXCERPTS FROM H. H. THOMAS'S *PRUNING MADE EASY*

FOREWORD

———— • ————

THE subject covered in this book is here largely as a result of many requests from those who have used my first book, "How to Prune Western Shrubs." I have hesitated in having this book printed because I was aware that this subject has been well covered many times by others, and in much greater detail.

Therefore, in publishing this book I have tried to make my instructions as simple as possible, to try to unmask the subject of "Pruning Fruit Trees," and put it in its correct light, that is, a very simple procedure, providing one knows what he is pruning for. In each type of fruit tree discussed, I have attempted to bring out the main reason why that particular tree needs pruning, in as simple a manner as I knew. To one who understands how, where, and why a tree bears its fruit, pruning is an extremely simple job.

This book is not intended for the commercial orchardist in any way. In fact in some cases the procedure which I have recommended is quite contrary to general orchard practice. The owner of a few trees for home consumption alone is not concerned with picking costs, maximum trees per acre, and mechanical cultivation problems. In many homes the fruit trees are neglected because no experienced pruner is at hand at the time the pruning should be done, and again, the price paid to have one or two trees pruned is out of proportion to the amount of fruit harvested.

It has not been my intention to make expert pruners out of everyone owning a fruit tree, but I hope that I may help those who have the desire and time to care for their own trees, thereby eliminating much unnecessary neglect and destruction by incorrect treatment.

R. SANFORD MARTIN.

HOW TO PRUNE FRUIT TREES

ALMOND

Almonds and Peaches are of the same family, but the Almond develops more erect type of growth, so must be kept thinned out more carefully. The method of fruit production is also slightly different, so that heading back of the fruit-bearing wood is unnecessary as is the case with Peaches.

Pruning should be done during the winter months while the tree is dormant.

In some sections of the country there will be more dieback than in other areas. The first procedure is to remove any dead wood which has shown up during the past season. Second, cut out the least important of interfering or rubbing branches.

Fruit will be borne on an Almond tree on the one-year branches. That is, branches which grew during the last season's growing period will produce fruit this summer.

Prune out the twigs which produced fruit the last summer, leaving one or two new shoots which should have grown from near the base of the last year's fruiting-wood. Make the cut immediately above the upper shoot to be left. These shoots or twigs, which are left will be the best fruit producing wood. When this phase of the pruning is complete, the tree should have an even distribution of young branches all over the tree. If they are thicker in one portion of the tree top than another, do a little further thinning until the distribution of one-year branches is even.

Do not be concerned about your Almond tree growing too tall, as the ripe nuts may be knocked from the branches with long poles without damage to the tree.

Because of the brittle characteristic of Almond wood, it is desirable to encourage the growth to be erect, with the center of the tree well filled in.

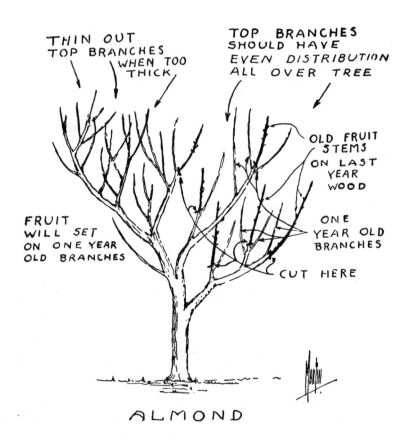

THIN OUT
TOP BRANCHES
WHEN TOO
THICK

TOP BRANCHES
SHOULD HAVE
EVEN DISTRIBUTION
ALL OVER TREE

OLD FRUIT
STEMS
ON LAST
YEAR
WOOD

FRUIT
WILL SET
ON ONE YEAR
OLD BRANCHES

ONE
YEAR OLD
BRANCHES

CUT HERE

ALMOND

APPLES

There is no set type for the shape of a bearing Apple tree, because, depending upon variety, the younger trees will vary from growing erect and slender to open and spreading. Eventually as the tree matures, it will develop into a fine spreading type. Observe your particular tree and if it is of the narrow erect type, according to its initial growth, make your pruning cuts just above buds which are pointed away from the center of the tree. If your variety of Apple is of the spreading type make the cuts above buds pointed toward the center of the tree. The time for pruning is during the winter months.

All Apples produce their fruit on "spurs," which are formed on the branches one year old or more, usually in the lower portion of these branches. These "spurs" are developed from the short lateral growths that vary in length from one to three inches. After they have definitely formed they can be recognized by their thick stubby appearance. The spurs produce blossoms and fruit year after year, and should be saved wherever possible.

When pruning the Apple tree, first cut out any dead or deceased branches, being careful to make cuts close to the main branch, without leaving any stub. This is very important because all apples are quite susceptible to rot, which can easily start in a stub which is left long enough to die back, rather than heal over with bark and new wood growth.

Second, cut away any interfering wood, or branches that are rubbing against one another, or that have come down too close to the ground and hinder cultivation.

Third, cut out sufficient of the last year's branch growth to evenly space all branches, allowing even sunlight penetration throughout the tree top. In doing this cutting, be careful to leave all established fruit spurs and those small

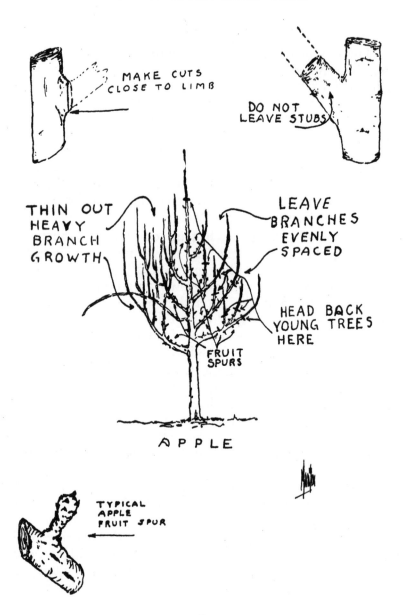

MAKE CUTS CLOSE TO LIMB

DO NOT LEAVE STUBS

THIN OUT HEAVY BRANCH GROWTH

LEAVE BRANCHES EVENLY SPACED

HEAD BACK YOUNG TREES HERE

FRUIT SPURS

APPLE

TYPICAL APPLE FRUIT SPUR

lateral bud developments that are to be future fruit spurs.

If the tree is making a normally rapid growth, especially a young tree, the new branch growth must be cut off just above the fruit spur buds. In the case of young trees, this will mean about two-thirds their length, as shown in the illustration.

Water sprouts or suckers should be cut out at any time that it is proven by their growth to be such. A sucker is a rapid growing shoot that comes from below ground, and they should be removed as soon as they appear, by digging down to their base and cutting them off very close to the root or trunk. Painting the cuts will help prevent rot from setting in. Water sprouts are "above ground suckers" and are recognized by their habit of growth, which is excessive in comparison with the rest of the branch growth of the tree. This growth is by nature, weak in structure and will not develop into suitable fruit producing wood, so cut it off clean and allow its sap to flow into more useful branches. These water sprouts, where allowed to grow will deprive the tree of valuable energy.

In the case of old trees, which have lost a main branch, or become one-sided, the water sprouts may be utilized to fill in vacant spaces, by heading them back, thereby forcing them to branch out and slow down their excessive soft growth.

Thinning the crop of fruit is frequently necessary with Apples, and this work should be done after the "June drop" has taken place. The "June drop" is a natural process with all fruit trees, in an effort by nature to adjust the crop to what the tree can bear. This period is apt to occur any time after the first of May, to July, and if in your opinion there still remains too much fruit for your trees to ripen, they may be hand thinned, leaving the remaining fruit evenly spaced throughout the tree's branches.

19

As the Apple tree takes on age there will be less and less pruning required. Give the tree its proper training in the first few years of its growth, and this will insure less care as it grows older.

APRICOTS

Like all other types of deciduous trees, the Apricot should be pruned during the dormant period or winter months, while the sap is inactive and the leaves are off the branches.

Apricots may be divided into three classes according to their fruit producing habits. In all cases the majority of the fruit is borne on one year old wood. Fruit may appear towards the tips of this growth, in the central section or in the lower section, and the fruiting habit of your tree may be ascertained by noting where the fattest buds are located on the one year old branches. The fattest or fullest buds are the flower producing buds, and indicate where the fruit will be set. The more slender buds will produce leaves and branch growth only.

In the case of the fruit buds being borne on the tip section, as is found in the "Royal" variety, do not head back the one year branches. In the case of the best fruit buds being in the central section, the one year growth may be headed back about one-third, and in the case of the fruit buds being in the lower branch section, the one year wood may be headed back from one-half to two-thirds of their length. The first type will apply in most cases, and in the event you can not determine in which class your tree belongs it would be advisable to prune your tree as though it were of the first type and do not head back the one year branches.

All varieties of Apricots maintain the same general habit of tree growth and the same pruning rules apply to all of them. Prune out enough branches to evenly shape the top, selecting old wood wherever possible, and in doing this so space the branch growth to allow even sunlight penetration to all parts of the fruit producing top. The long whip-like branches which grew during last summer is the fruit pro-

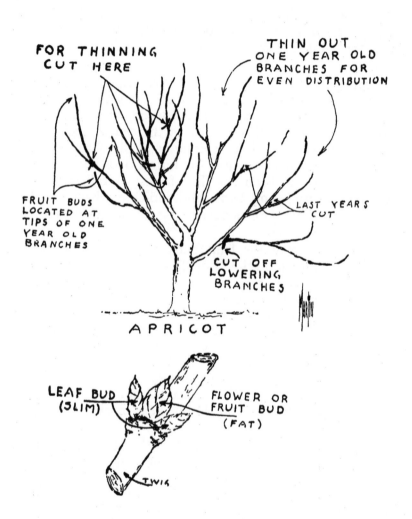

FOR THINNING
CUT HERE

THIN OUT
ONE YEAR OLD
BRANCHES FOR
EVEN DISTRIBUTION

FRUIT BUDS
LOCATED AT
TIPS OF ONE
YEAR OLD
BRANCHES

LAST YEARS
CUT

CUT OFF
LOWERING
BRANCHES

APRICOT

LEAF BUD
(SLIM)

FLOWER OR
FRUIT BUD
(FAT)

TWIG

22

ducing wood for the coming year, so don't cut it too freely, and do not head back any of these branches unless the tree is of the second or third type as mentioned above.

The outside branches of the Apricot have a tendency to gradually lower each year, with the weight of fruit and foliage, and as these branches get low enough to interfere with cultivation, etc., they may be cut off without any damage to the tree. The nature of the tree is to replace these lowering outside branches with inside central growth, and these growths should be cared for as part of the original tree, and their development encouraged.

For the first four or five years of an Apricot tree's growth, its development is very rapid, and therefore their training is most important. Read the chapter on Training of Young Trees, and govern your trees accordingly.

Some varieties of Apricots will develop fruit spurs on the older wood, and wherever they appear they should be left because their fruit is always strong and well developed.

Because the Apricot wood is of a brittle nature, care should be taken not to allow any one branch or branches to spread laterally too great a distance. This practice encourages breakage of limbs. Favor erect growth wherever possible. A sturdy framework on your tree is much to be desired, even at the expense of early fruit production. A well spaced, husky framework of branches will have less tendency to branch breakage under an abnormally heavy crop, than a tree that has been allowed to grow undirected.

AVOCADOS

There is no fruit grown which has developed more different schools of thought regarding correct pruning, than has the Avocado. The writer has witnessed the practice and results of various methods used in commercial plantings of this fruit, and when they are consistently carried out, give satisfactory results as far as fruit production and harvesting is concerned. However, as this book is devoted to the production of fruit on a small scale such as the average home with one or more Avocado trees, instructions shall be confined to methods believed most practical to this small scale production, where economy of harvesting is not an item to be considered.

One of the first things to be remembered with Avocados, is that in its natural habitat the tree grows in semi-tropic forests and, therefore, the more nearly we can reproduce such a growing condition the more success we shall have.

First, because of their natural home being in forests, the trees have developed the characteristic of the feeding roots being very close to the surface of the ground, which in the forest would be covered by a thick carpet of fallen leaves. Therefore, reproduce this condition as nearly as possible with decaying vegetation, such as bean straw or leaves, or dried grass, but never allow growing grasses over the roots.

Second, natural forests are not cultivated, hence the feeder roots close to the surface. Cultivation renders surface roots useless, which frequently results in the dropping of fruit in any stage of development. Consequently, mulch your Avocado trees well and don't cultivate.

As far as fruit production is concerned the Avocado needs no pruning, but because of the weak nature of branch wood, heavy leaves and fruit, the outer branches will

24

AVOCADO

constantly be lowering year after year until they are touching the ground. These lowering branches should be removed gradually so as not to produce a "hole" in the tree's foliage which might allow sunburn of the inner branch bark.

It is the nature of the primary, or bright green, bark on the main trunk and branches to sunburn unless well protected by the foliage. This sunburn hardens the bark and slows down the sap activity to such an extent that it makes a difficult condition to overcome without expert attention. In young trees, where a main branch or stem has become sunburned from exposure, try to encourage a new branch from below the affected area to grow in place of the sunburned branch.

If your tree grows one-sided, as is frequently the case with backyard Avocados, head back the tip growth gradually, on the heavy side of the tree, thereby forcing growth in other portions. As your trees reach mature growth their one-sidedness will be eliminated naturally.

Pruning may be done whenever lowering branches make it necessary. Die-back branches on inside of tree should be cut out as they appear. The older the tree the less the trimming that will be needed.

BOYSENBERRY   YOUNGBERRY
LOGANBERRY   BLACKBERRY
DEWBERRY   VICTORBERRY

•

There are many varieties of the bramble fruits that will respond to one system of pruning because of their similar habit of producing fruit. Namely, those that produce their fruit on one year old canes.

None of the above listed types will require pruning the first year they are planted. Pruning will begin the second winter after planting.

The first summer the plants may be allowed to sprawl on the ground at will, because there will be no fruit on this first summer's growth, and the sprawling canes will provide some measure of insulation or protection of the soil around the roots.

During the first winter a trellis or frame must be built on which to place the now fully matured canes. Any one of several types of frame may be used, but perhaps the easiest to build will be a simple, three-wire fence-type of frame. The first wire should be about one and a half feet above the ground, next wire one foot above the first, and the top wire one foot above the second. The wires should be lined up directly over the row, or series of hills where the vines have been planted. Be sure that the end posts are firmly set and braced as they must support considerable weight each summer. The wire may be tightened during the winter after the season's cutting back has been done and the wires are free of weight.

Once the wires are stretched the berry canes which grew the previous summer and now are sprawling on the

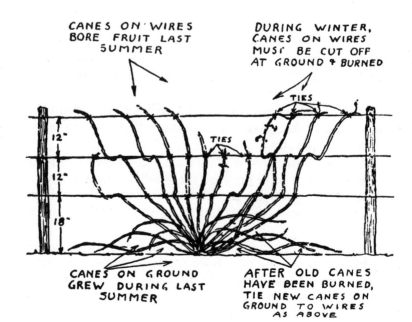

CANES ON WIRES
BORE FRUIT LAST
SUMMER

DURING WINTER,
CANES ON WIRES
MUST BE CUT OFF
AT GROUND & BURNED

TIES

TIES

12"

12"

18"

CANES ON GROUND
GREW DURING LAST
SUMMER

AFTER OLD CANES
HAVE BEEN BURNED,
TIE NEW CANES ON
GROUND TO WIRES
AS ABOVE

PRUNING SYSTEM FOR
BOYSENBERRY - YOUNGBERRY - LOGANBERRY
BLACKBERRY - DEWBERRY - VICTORBERRY
AND OTHERS.

ground, should be tied up on the wires. In doing this, take care to spread the canes evenly on the wires so that it will be easy to pick the berries. Wherever possible it is advisable to twine the cane once around the wire before tying with a soft string. Never use wire for tying.

The pruning which will be necessary every winter on established berry vines, is simple in its routine. First, go down the row cutting out all of the old canes which are tied on the wires. A pair of long handled shears may be used so that the old canes may be cut off at the ground level without too much bending down. After the old canes have been cut off, they should be cleared away and burned. The next procedure is to tie up the new crop of canes that sprawl on the ground and which grew during the past summer.

In tying up these canes it will be easier to start with those which have made the shorter growth, training these in a more vertical position, twining the cane once around each wire as you reach it. It will be necessary to use string only near the tip of the cane, just to hold it in position. Be careful not to bend a cane too sharply, as they are apt to break.

After the short canes are tied up the longer ones may be trained out fanwise, in such a spacing that the finished job will show an even distribution of canes on the wires. The more evenly the canes are spread on the wires, the better the sunlight penetration to the ripening fruit, which contributes to the sweetness of the berries.

The main thing to remember in the pruning of these types of berry fruits, is that fruit is borne on canes which have grown through one summer. After this growth has produced one crop of fruit it will not set another satisfactory crop, even though it were left on the plant. When the old canes are cut out, cut them off at ground level. The new shoots will appear as suckers from below ground. Allow all of them to grow, except those that appear as suckers out away from the main hill or row.

This type of berry plant is a heavy feeder and likes a moist condition for its roots. Organic manures will be best for fertilizing during the winter.

CHERRY

The most important part of the pruning of a Cherry tree is in the training that the tree receives during its first four or five years after setting out. If the training has been properly done during this period, the mature tree will require very little attention from then on in the way of pruning.

This primary care is more important with the sweet varieties of Cherries, than with the sour types, because all of the Sweet Cherries are naturally very tall growers, and are inclined to develop very weak crotches when allowed to retain all of their top growth. This pruning method is to promote a strong framework tree, rather than for increased fruit production. Pruning should be done during winter months.

When the Cherry tree is first planted out it is usually a straight whip with no lateral branches, so at the time of planting, this whip should be cut off, or headed, at about twenty-five (25) inches above ground. This takes care of its first pruning, and as the new growth starts out select three shoots in the top eighteen inches of growth, about six inches apart up and down the stem, as shown in the chapter devoted to the "Training of Young Trees." Keep all other lateral shoots rubbed off, allowing all of the strength to go into these three framework branches.

Next year cut back these three framework branches to about one-third to one-half their season's-growth length, and during the following summer select two well spaced shoots to develop on each of the three framework branches, rubbing off any other laterals as they appear.

The next season repeat the directions of the last paragraph selecting two shoots on each of the previous year's growth, and continue as above until the tree is four or five years old. From this point on the tree will practically take care of itself, with the exception of removing any branches which are interfering with other limbs, always removing the branch which is least desirable to the general shape of the tree.

Sour Cherries will only require the training period for three years, and thereafter it will be necessary to thin out the top, or fruiting wood, every winter, because of the nature of the bearing wood to grow into a tangle of small branches. In doing this thinning, cut out enough of the twig growth to eliminate a tangled appearance, and so that the branches are evenly spaced throughout the top.

CURRANTS

The most satisfactory way to grow Currants for fruit production is by the bush method, where you have an opportunity to renew the fruiting wood. This system is extremely simple, and is perfectly natural for the plant.

The main thing to remember in the pruning of Currants is that a cane that develops from the base of the plant, will produce a good crop of fruit for three seasons, and from then on the quality and amount of fruit produced on this same cane will decrease. To take advantage of this natural characteristic of the plant, one should cut out any canes after they have produced three successive crops of fruit. In making these cuts, follow down the cane to its base and cut the whole growth out, leaving a short stub above the ground about four inches long.

If there is a new, strong growth coming up, near the base of the cane to be cut out, make your cut just above this shoot, so that it will receive all the strength that formerly went into the old wood.

The best time of year to do this pruning will be the winter months, although in the milder climates, summer pruning may be done where there is not the danger of the plant's suffering from "winter kill." For general practice, however, the dormant season or winter pruning is recommended.

A mature Currant plant will carry twelve good strong canes with their branches, and it is advisable to limit the plants to this amount of top growth. This limiting may be done by cutting back any greater number of canes as they start their spring and early summer growth, always leaving the strongest new canes.

In the event that the canes of Currants become infested with borers, which will be noticed by a generally unhealthy appearance of the entire cane, cut that cane out completely and burn it to prevent the infestation from spreading to the remainder of the plant or neighboring bushes.

For illustration covering the pruning of Currants, follow the one used for Gooseberries. The pruning system is identical.

ESPALIER TRAINING

This method of training fruit trees, as well as many types of ornamental shrubs, has long been practiced in various parts of the world, and is now becoming more and more popular in this country. Where this work is done well, it is very interesting, and adds to the artistic arrangement of a landscape planting.

This article will deal only with the fundamental practice of Espalier work, rather than confine the instructions to the development of any one form or shape of frame. The shape to which the plant is to be trained will vary according to the location in which it is to be used.

Because the training of any Espalier may spread over several years, it might be better to sketch a design to be followed, suitable to the location, and then keep this sketch on file for ready reference.

The variety of plant to be used should be decided between yourself and your nurseryman, so as to obtain the best results. The selection of the individual plant is very important. Choose one that already has branches located in such distribution along the stem as to be easily trained to the basic framework of the Espalier. Where deciduous plants are to be used, the work should be started during the dormant season, because with most plants, the branches are less brittle during this time of year.

Fast growing plants are not the best to use, because they are too difficult to confine to the limits of an Espaliered design. Make your selection from a variety of plant which produces stocky branches with abundant leaves, flowers or fruit.

Care should be taken also in the selection of the variety. Choose a type of plant that will produce flowers or fruit on the same branches indefinitely. The Pear tree is an ex-

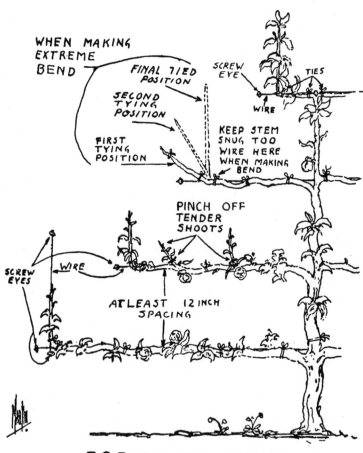

WHEN MAKING
EXTREME
BEND

FINAL TIED
POSITION

SECOND
TYING
POSITION

FIRST
TYING
POSITION

SCREW
EYE

TIES

WIRE

KEEP STEM
SNUG TOO
WIRE HERE
WHEN MAKING
BEND

PINCH OFF
TENDER
SHOOTS

SCREW
EYES

WIRE

AT LEAST 12 INCH
SPACING

ESPALLIER TRAINING

cellent example, because once its fruit spurs are developed on the branches they will produce blossoms and fruit on the same wood year after year.

The primary training of any Espaliered plant is of the utmost importance because once a branch is bent to a desired position and tied firmly there for a period of at least one year, it will remain in that position throughout the life of the plant. Be very exacting in the primary training.

In the initial training a great deal of care should be exercised in doing the bending and tying. Where it is necessary to make a complete right-angle bend, the branch will not stand such a radical change in direction all at once without danger of breaking. To avoid this possible destruction it will be necessary to bend the branch not more than one quarter of the complete bend, and leave it tied in this position for a period of two weeks to a month; then bend and tie a little more and leave for another period of two weeks to a month; keeping this up until the complete bend has been accomplished. Before starting any bends be sure that the branch is tied firmly immediately below the bend, as this will help in maintaining a more symmetrical Espalier.

In order to maintain an Espalier in proper order it will be necessary to do some minor pruning all through the growing period, by removing any new growth that appears in undesirable locations and favoring growth which may be used for further training or fruit production.

Summer pruning is necessary to keep the plant confined to its framework, and when this work is done do not trim out the entire young shoot, instead pinch off the tender tip of the shoot which will stop its length growth and develop the closely set buds and leaves which are at the base of any new twig growth.

When an Espalier is first started it is usually a temptation to develop the main framework branches too close

37

together. Remember that the plant is going to be there for many years, and that as it grows the growth is going to get coarser, so if the framework branches are trained about 12 inches apart the finished effect will always be about right.

Espaliered plants may be very beautiful in effect when properly cared for, but when they do not receive the proper attention they present a most unkempt condition. If one is willing to give an Espaliered plant a few minutes attention every month *regularly,* he may have some very beautiful plants trained in this system.

In the case of fruits such as Pears and Plums, which produce fruit on the same spurs year after year, do not prune the spurs out, as they never attain great length and may always be counted upon for flowers and fruit, as well as leaves.

It will be necessary to check up on your tying several times during the growing season because as a branch expands the tie becomes tighter, and if not renewed from time to time, may completely choke off the circulation of sap in the branch. The best material to use for tying is a soft fiber cord, or cloth tape. Never use wire as this not only bruises the bark of a branch but is more difficult to undo for retying.

FEIJOA OR PINEAPPLE GUAVA

Like many of the subtropical plants, this one bears its fruit on current season, or new wood. Therefore one must be very careful not to do any heading back when pruning.

The best time of year to do any necessary pruning is just after the fruit has all fallen from the tree. About all that will be needed is a thinning out of interfering branches or to remove any limbs which might be rubbing one another.

The natural growing habit of a Feijoa is that of a large semi-spreading shrub, and it is a mistake to attempt to force the plant into any other form by the practice of external hedging, because in so doing, the fruiting possibilities will be largely destroyed.

When the fruit of the Feijoa is ripe it will fall to the ground, where it should be harvested. Never attempt to pick the fruit from the tree.

As the plant grows it will become necessary to re-shape its growth from time to time, by encouraging the growth of new branches in the center of the head, because a heavy crop will often distort the branches. Lowering branches also must be pruned off as they drop too low.

FIGS
White — Brown — Black

Figs may be divided into two classes regarding their pruning. In the first group would be the white and brown figs, which require heavy annual pruning, and the second group would be the black figs which with their different habit of fruit production require other treatment.

SYSTEM NUMBER ONE
White and Brown Figs

(vs. Kadota, Thompson, Brown Turkey, White Pacific, Adriatic, etc.)

These varieties produce their best fruit on current season's wood, or that is, they bear fruit this year on branches which are produced and growing this year.

Because of this, the branches which were produced during the past summer should be cut back heavily during the dormant period or winter months.

In this pruning system, the branches should be cut back to two bud spurs. Or, cut the branch off about a half inch above the second bud or leaf scar from the base of the branch.

If the tree is in normal health and vigor, each one of the two buds will put out growth in the spring, which in turn will produce figs during the summer, and in the following dormant period these branches must be cut back as described above. This system of heavy pruning is needed every year.

In the case of a newly planted tree, it will be advisable to start it out with a fairly low head, or crotch. The best type tree to plant should be a single "whip," with possibly a few lateral branches. When the tree is planted, therefore,

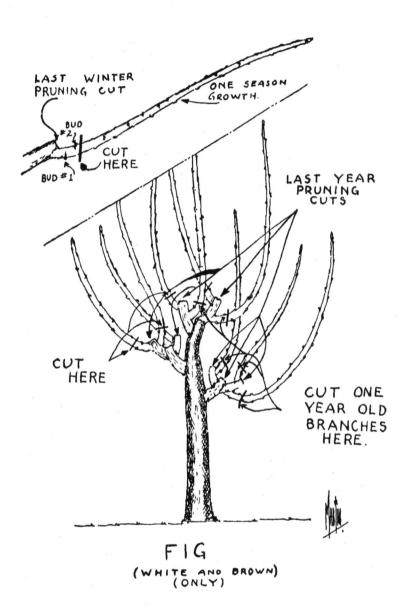

LAST WINTER
PRUNING CUT

ONE SEASON
GROWTH.

BUD
#2

CUT
HERE

BUD #1

LAST YEAR
PRUNING
CUTS

CUT
HERE

CUT ONE
YEAR OLD
BRANCHES
HERE.

FIG
(WHITE AND BROWN)
(ONLY)

41

it should be cut off at a height of 20 to 24 inches above the ground. Then do not allow more than three new branches to grow during the first season. Select three branches that are evenly spaced around the trunk. (See instructions on "Training of Young Trees.")

The better figs will be produced on the fast growing branches which will result from this heavy cutting back. If the tree is allowed to go untrimmed, the fruit will be of inferior size and quality. A normal young tree will frequently put out many new branches which will grow from six to eight feet during a summer and produce a fig at practically every leaf base or axis.

SYSTEM NUMBER TWO
Black Figs
(vs. Mission, San Pedro, etc.)

This type of fig produces fruit on wood that is one year old and older, so an eitirely different system of pruning must be followed in order to get fruit production.

The black fig, when planted out should be headed, or cut back to about two feet from the ground in order to induce a rapid first year's "framework" growth. Three branches will be enough for the tree to support during the first summer. Don't expect any figs the first year.

If your black fig tree is to be used as a combination shade tree and fruit producer, it may be headed higher to allow for its spreading branches higher off the ground, and in such a case, cut the top off at about four feet from the ground.

After the tree has made its first summer's growth, all the winter pruning that is needed will be to thin out any interfering or rubbing branches, and see to it that the top is kept evenly spaced.

Because all figs are inclined to "bleed" profusely when cut while the sap is active, the pruning should take place during the dormant period only, in the winter months while no leaves are on the branches.

Any kind of grass, such as lawn, growing over the feeder roots of figs, as well as other fruit trees, will have a tendency to deprive the fruit of its full amount of sugar, so maintain a cultivated area beneath the tree that is slightly larger than the total diameter of the top spread.

GOOSEBERRIES

This variety of fruit is one which takes care of itself to a certain extent, but the quality of fruit may be greatly improved if the bushes are regularly pruned every winter, after the plants are four years old. The reason for this wait being that a branch will bear good fruit for three years, after attaining one full year's growth, but after it has borne for three seasons the quality and size of the berries will decrease, therefore the necessity of pruning.

Because Gooseberries will produce to some extent on the same branches year after year, without pruning, it is very easy to understand why this plant is sometimes so neglected.

When a branch starts its growth from the base of the plant it requires one full season of growing before it is sufficiently mature to produce fruit.

The pruning procedure to follow is to allow this cane to stay on the bush during three fruiting periods and then cut it out to make way for new bearing wood. On taking out the branch, make the cut well down to the base of the plant, leaving a stub of from six to seven inches in length upon which new shoots will sprout. The pruning should be done during the winter months.

The following spring there may be many new shoots which will start out from the stub, but allow only about three of the strongest to grow. Pull the others off while they are still soft.

Although it may be a temptation to leave all of the fruit-producing branches, a well established plant will produce about so many pounds of fruit and it is better to have this poundage in large sized fruit rather than a great abundance of undersized berries. This system of pruning will insure the right type of wood on the bush that will produce the largest berries possible.

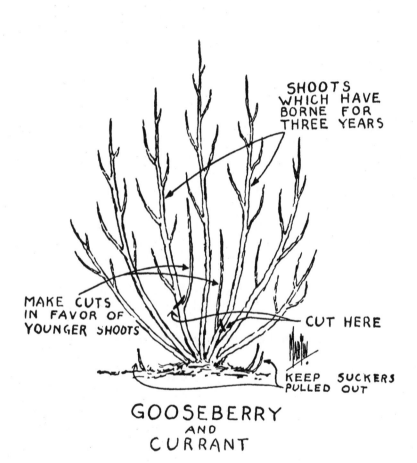

SHOOTS
WHICH HAVE
BORNE FOR
THREE YEARS

MAKE CUTS
IN FAVOR OF
YOUNGER SHOOTS

CUT HERE

KEEP SUCKERS
PULLED OUT

GOOSEBERRY
AND
CURRANT

45

GRAPEFRUIT *or Pomelo*

Like many of the citrus trees, there is little to be done to a Grapefruit tree as far as pruning is concerned. Under average conditions it will not be necessary to prune the tree at all until it is at least five years old, because their growth is always very uniform in its habits, and the tree will practically shape itself.

The only pruning that might be necessary on a young Grapefruit tree is to remove any rubbing or crossing branches. Where branches of citrus trees have an opportunity to rub against one another causing a breaking of the bark, it makes it very easy for disease to start from such a wound. In removing a rubbing or crossing branch, cut out the one which contributes the least to the general shape of the tree.

Because of the extremely dense habit of growth of the Grapefruit as time goes on, there will always be a certain amount of dead twigs on the inside of the tree head. These should be cut off, smooth to the living branch, so that the die-back will not travel into the living branches. This cutting out of the dead twigs should be attended to about twice a year, six months apart. In this way the twig will be cut off before it has died completely to the main branch, which will allow the cut to heal better.

As the Grapefruit develops size there will be less and less foliage on the inside of the tree head, so it will be easier to see what pruning will be needed by standing on the inside of the tree. There will usually be room enough in between the branches to move one's arms around sufficiently to do the necessary thinning out. By standing on the ground with your head and body inside the head of the tree, one may notice where the branches are growing more dense in some spots than in others, and these overly thick collections of

46

twig growth should be thinned out to allow a slight penetration of sunlight. This work requires the thinning out of only small twigs, because large "holes" should not be opened up suddenly by heavier pruning.

This pruning may be done at any time of the year, because by following this system, it will probably not be necessary to cut out any actual fruit-bearing wood. However, pruning during the winter, or cool weather, would be better for the tree.

Do not allow any branches to hang down to within one foot of the ground, as this makes it more possible for various fungus diseases to infect any low hanging fruit which might be borne on them.

GRAPES

There are two general types of Grapes, namely bush and vine. Their respective systems of pruning will be taken up separately. Also because either one may be grown for fruit production alone, or as an arbor plant, the pruning system for each type will be taken up individually.

BUSH TYPE GRAPES

(Such as Muscat, Malaga, Thompson Seedless, Tokay, etc.)

Grown for fruit production only.

The first year that the grape is planted out should be devoted to training only. Place a vertical stake by the plant so that there is two feet of stake above ground and allow only one cane to grow by selecting the strongest and cutting off all other lateral or side shoots which may start. This will force all of the season's growth into the one cane which may be tied at intervals to the stake to keep the stem straight. When the one cane reaches the top of the stake, tie it firmly and allow it to sprawl around at will for the rest of the growing period.

During the winter the main cane should be cut off, about two inches above the top of the stake. In the spring when the new growth starts, allow only the two top buds, or joints, to send out shoots. Cut off smooth with the side of the branch, any shoots which appear on what may now be called the trunk, or stem.

Through the summer growing season allow these two shoots, or canes, to make whatever growth they will, without further training or pruning. There may or may not be some grapes set on this growth. If they do set, the plant will be strong enough to ripen them, so they may be left.

Now will begin the regular annual system which must

48

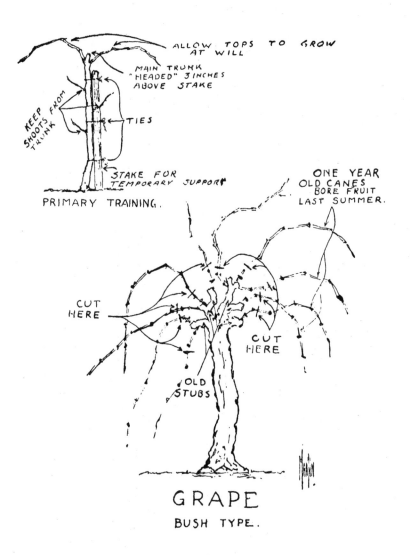

ALLOW TOPS TO GROW
AT WILL

MAIN TRUNK
"HEADED" 3 INCHES
ABOVE STAKE

KEEP SHOOTS FROM TRUNK

TIES

STAKE FOR
TEMPORARY SUPPORT

PRIMARY TRAINING.

ONE YEAR
OLD CANES
BORE FRUIT
LAST SUMMER.

CUT
HERE

CUT
HERE

OLD
STUBS

GRAPE
BUSH TYPE.

49

be followed every winter. The preceding instructions cover the initial training period only.

During the winter season while the grape is dormant is the time that the pruning should be done. All canes that grew the past summer must be cut back to just above the second bud or joint from the base of the one year old canes. There will always be a group of latent buds right at the base of the cane, which will only be forced in case the other buds are damaged in some way. Count out from the base of the cane, two buds or joints and cut the cane off about a half inch beyond the second bud.

If the plant is strong, both of these buds will start growing in the spring, and if they do, leave them. The bunches of grapes will appear on this new growth which has started from the short stubs that were left.

Be sure to do the pruning as soon as possible in the fall after the leaves have all dropped, because at this time there is no sap activity and the canes will not bleed as a result of being cut.

As soon as the trunk is large enough to support itself, do away with the stake, and do not rely on further support or tying.

BUSH TYPE GRAPES FOR ARBORS

There are no set rules which must be followed as to any particular type of trellis or arbor for grape training. Grapes will adapt themselves to almost any type of screen or arbor, providing they get plenty of sun for ripening their fruit.

When growing grapes for arbors, the initial training is of all-importance and should be attended to at least once every two weeks through the growing period. A grape arbor will produce its best fruit on top, so it will be inadvisable to try to maintain any fruit production on the sides. For this reason force all the growth into one main cane which is to be trained vertically up the side of the arbor. This main cane may be either twined around the upright post or tied to it. Discourage any lateral growth along this main stem by rubbing off any side buds as they appear.

As soon as the vine has reached the top of the arbor, the fruit producing wood may be developed. The canes should either be twined around the supporting wire or trellis in fanwise or parallel form, keeping any parallel canes about twelve or fifteen inches apart. This growth will be the permanent framework from which the fruit will be produced every year for an indefinite period, so be very careful and exacting with the training of the permanent canes. Do not try to get fruit production from any cane until it has made its full growth as foundation wood. It may take several seasons to get full coverage from the foundation wood. However, as any one foundation cane reaches its full development, the pruning for fruit production may begin the following winter.

Once the canes are established, they will begin to put out fruit producing wood the following year. These permanent canes will produce fruit year after year indefinitely when properly pruned.

The pruning procedure to follow is very simple. During the winter months, as soon as the leaves have dried and fallen, cut back all of the canes which grew during the past summer, including those which produced fruit. Cut them back to within two buds or joints above their base. New fruit bearing canes will grow from one or both of the buds which were left.

As time goes on the framework branches will become very heavy, with increasing size, but this condition will not affect the fruiting possibilities of the vine. As long as the annual wood is renewed systematically each year, the vine will produce good sized bunches indefinitely.

51

VINING TYPE GRAPES
(Such as Eastern Concord, etc.)

This type of grape includes those more immediately descended from the wild grapes of the woods, and they are all natural climbers, therefore requiring a specific treatment in order to obtain the best production from them.

There have been many systems of training developed for these grapes, some of them quite complicated. The simplest form of training, and one which will assure the grower of a good yield with the least amount of work, is the one referred to as the "two arm Cordon" system, which includes the construction of a three wire "fence" type of trellis.

The construction of this type trellis should be done with an eye to the future; that is, do not use light materials for the end posts and their bracing. The posts and wires must support a great deal of weight as years go by, so sturdy construction is a definite economy.

Where a three wire trellis is used, which by the way will give the most satisfactory support for the vines, the lower wire should be stretched tight, two feet from the ground. The second wire one foot above the lower, and the third, or top wire, one foot above the second.

The young vines should be planted ten feet apart, directly under the wires, and then the training may commence as the vines grow. If the following training is done carefully for the first few years it will greatly simplify the pruning in future years. Each vine can be trained into an almost exact duplicate of all the others.

As the young vine grows, it may be held in place with a light vertical stake until it gets up to about the height of the first wire, then this temporary stake may be removed and the first arm of the cordon started on its training. When the growth starts in the spring, select *one* good strong shoot which has forced out from the base of last year's growth.

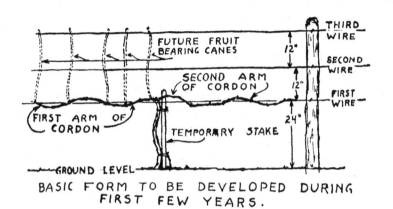

BASIC FORM TO BE DEVELOPED DURING
FIRST FEW YEARS.

VINING TYPE GRAPES

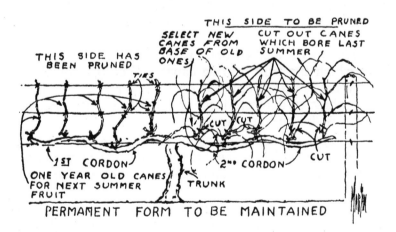

PERMANENT FORM TO BE MAINTAINED

Cut off all other shoots, forcing *all* of the growth into one sturdy cane. Do not even allow any lateral or side shoots to grow from the one cane until the first or lowest wire is reached. Then if a shoot develops at this level it may be used for training the second arm of the cordon.

Just as soon as the young shoot is long enough to twine around the first wire, start in the training by twining it out around the wire. This initial training may go on for two or three years, depending upon the growth that the plant makes. Keep up the training of this first cane until the tip has reached a point five feet out on the wire, then pinch off the tip or terminal bud, to stop its horizontal growth.

In the meantime the training may be started on the arm in the opposite direction, by allowing, as previously mentioned, a bud to grow, which has started at about the point where the main trunk meets the lower wire. Train this cane, as with the other one, until it has reached a point five feet from the main stem in the opposite direction.

Now there should be the main stem or trunk and the two arms of the cordon stretching in opposite directions, supported by the lower wire, forming a T with a broad top bar.

This "two armed cordon" is the permanent framework from which the fruit bearing canes will be developed year after year. Where pruning is done properly, each joint or bud on these cordons produces fruit bearing canes each year as long as the vine survives.

This type of grape produces fruit from the first three to five joints, or buds, on canes which have grown during the previous summer. This same cane will not produce fruit again.

Allow the canes which spring out on each arm to grow as they wish during the summer, without any tying. During the winter dormant period, select about five of the strongest, one year old canes, on each arm, and tie them vertically to the two wires above. For this purpose use either twine or annealed iron wire of very fine gauge. Never use copper wire. The fine iron wire is usually so rusted from being in the weather that it breaks very easily when it comes time to prune off the canes which it has held up for the past year. Cut the tied canes about three inches above the top wire.

All other canes which have grown from the arm should now be cut back, leaving two buds above their base.

Each cane which has been tied in this manner, should produce about three bunches of grapes of good size, and with ten canes tied, will mean about thirty bunches of grapes for each vine.

The next winter remove the canes which are tied up, cutting them off just above one good strong shoot which has grown from its base. After the last year's fruit canes have been removed, tie up the new strong canes, as before, selecting five from each arm, and continue this treatment year after year.

Where treated right, the Concords and similar varieties, in California, have far out-produced their parent vineyards in the Eastern states, as well as producing a higher quality grape.

VINE TYPE GRAPES FOR ARBORS
Same training as for "bush type grapes for arbors."

GUAVAS — *Red or Yellow*

Like many of the subtropical fruits, the red or yellow Guavas require little in the way of pruning because of their fruiting habits. The fruit is borne on new wood.

The growth of these plants is very shrubby by nature, and because of this the bushes will require very little shaping. The only pruning necessary, therefore, is only that which the location of the plant might govern. Where Guavas have been used as ornamental plants, it may become necessary to trim out any branches which are growing out of bounds, too tall or too spreading.

The best time of year to do this pruning is in the winter months, while the plants are making little or no growth.

In the case of an old hedge of guavas that has grown too tall, and is rather unsightly, due to their open habit of growth, the plants may be cut back or de-horned heavily, and the hedge started all over again. In cutting of this sort, cut off all growth about two feet from the ground during the late winter months. This severe treatment may spoil one season's fruit production, but the plants will throw out masses of new shoots from the old stems, which will make a new low hedge of attractive appearance.

Pruning will not increase fruit production of the Guavas, therefore this work is a matter of individual plant shape.

LEMON

There are many systems for the pruning of Lemon trees, all of which have been worked out to apply to orchard conditions for various localities in which the fruit is grown, and they are proving successful wherever they are used consistently.

The system most easily adopted to the amateur grower of Lemons, where there are from one to three trees in a yard, is as follows, and is a system which takes advantage of the natural growing habit of the tree, and will require the least amount of attention. Because "cost of picking" does not enter into the amateur's lemon growing, this system will prove excellent.

Pruning may be done on a Lemon, where one uses the following system, at any time of the year when it becomes necessary, because lemons are flowering and fruiting constantly.

Under average circumstances a lemon tree will require no pruning for the first four years after it has been set out, except to trim out any branch which rubs against another, and to rub off any sucker shoots which might appear on the trunk or stem. In removing these shoots, it is better to rub them off or pull them, rather than cut them, because cutting encourages regrowth of more shoots.

The natural habit of a Lemon tree after it is well established is to send out long upright fast growing shoots from the center of the head, which in time become heavy at the tip with foliage and then begins to gradually bend down. This natural habit may be used to develop a very productive tree, and one which will have very large fruit, all during the year.

Like many citrus trees it is not advisable to allow any branches within about two feet from the ground, because of the danger of fungus infection of fruit, so as the lower branches are carried lower each year with the weight of fruit and foliage they may be cut off and that energy forced into the development of other branches. Cut these off well back into the head of the tree, where they leave a main limb. Make a smooth cut without leaving a stub. The stub encourages rot on the main limbs.

The long spindling upright shoots which appear during the summer months in the center of the tree, will in time make good fruiting wood, so they should be left, except where too many spring out in one place. In this case select one of the strongest and cut out the others. As these tall shoots reach the top of the tree they will begin to develop lateral twigs and heavy foliage, which will cause them to bend down in an arching habit. As they come down, remove any branches which might get in their way. As this wood matures it will begin to set fruit, and the Lemons nearest the ends of these branches are usually the finest quality.

This system of growing may be carried on indefinitely, constantly renewing the fruit bearing wood. The tree may not be the most symmetrical in shape, but it will be producing an abundance of high quality Lemons.

As the limbs get too close to the ground (2 feet), cut the branch out and develop new ones from the inside of the tree's head. From the time that one of these upright branches starts its growth to the time when it is necessary to be removed because it has grown too close to the ground, will be anywhere from five to ten years.

The dwarf bush Lemon will require practically no pruning, except to cut out any interfering branches, and as the limbs bend down to the ground, to cut them off well back inside the plant, which will force new growth in more desirable locations.

LIME

There are many species of Lime grown commercially, as well as in the backyard garden, but they all have the same requirements as far as pruning is concerned. As trees go, the Lime will shape itself into a very symmetrical top.

Any sucker growth that appears on the stem should be rubbed off as it appears. Where these shoots are allowed to grow, they will take most of the vitality which should go into the top.

Most Lime varieties develop a very dense leaf growth, which completely excludes the direct sunlight from the inside of the tree. This condition causes a considerable amount of die-back among the small twigs on the inside of the tree head. These dead twigs should be cut out about twice each year, for if left in them, they will encourage rot to enter the main limbs. In cutting them out, cut the dead or dying twig back smooth to a main branch. Do not leave even a short stub.

At the time that this die-back trimming is being done, watch out for any rubbing or crossing branches that may have grown in the top. Remove the one which contributes the least to the general good shape of the tree. The heaviest cutting should be done during the winter months, whenever neceessary.

LOQUAT

There are few fruit trees that require any less trimming than does the Loquat. In fact, this variety could grow very successfully with no pruning at all.

Loquat trees should be headed quite low when they are first set out, because as the tree develops it is a constant subdividing of terminal growth, causing the general shape of the tree to be an inverted pyramid.

The only pruning to be done is to cut out any dead branches and to pull off any sucker growth that appears below the head or from the roots.

As this fruit is a member of the Apple family, it is subject to "Pear Blight," a bacterial disease which attacks all of this family. The disease may be recognized by the sudden dying of twig tips and leaves, almost as though the leaves had been burned by fire. When this occurs, cut out the infected branch at least a foot beyond any show of infection. The disease travels in the sap, so it may be further down the twig than the leaves show. Cut far enough to be safe.

Loquat pruning should be done in early fall, so that the tree may fully recover before the fruit buds start to develop.

NECTARINE

This fruit being a very close relative of the Peach, the system of pruning is very similar, except that it will not be necessary to prune quite so heavily. The fruit is borne on one year old branches, not on spurs, so the fruiting wood must be renewed every season.

For training young Nectarine trees, see the chapter on "Training Young Trees."

The Nectarine, like the Peach, will set its best fruit in the center one-third section of one year old branches. Keep this fact in mind as the tree is shaped and pruned. Pruning must be done during the dormant period in winter.

When the pruning actually begins the procedure is as follows:

First, remove any dead or interfering wood from the tree top, along with any branches which bore fruit last year. All suckers on the stem should be removed as they appear during the summer.

Second, select the strongest branches with the most amount of lateral twig growth for the fruit producing wood. This twig growth is the fruiting wood for the coming season. Thin out any branches in such a way as to leave an evenly spaced branch-work in the top.

Third, thin out the fruiting twigs so that they are spaced about eight inches to one foot apart all over the tree.

Fourth, clip back all of the remaining fruiting twigs (one year old), one-third their length. This procedure will leave enough fruit buds for the tree to care for. Do not do any hand thinning of fruit until after the normal June drop has occurred. The tree will carry and mature all fruit left after this natural thinning process.

Avoid propping the limbs unless absolutely necessary.

In event the use of props is needed, however, remove them just as soon as the fruit is off the tree, because their continued use will cause a weakening of the branch structure.

For illustration governing the pruning of Nectarine, see the one covering pruning of Peaches. The fundamentals are the same.

PEACHES

There are few fruit trees that benefit from heavy pruning as does the Peach. The size and quality of the fruit is governed by whether or not the tree is properly pruned. This pruning to be done during the winter dormant period.

Peaches will stand, and be better for it, a heavier removal of old wood than any other fruit tree. Frequently it will be necessary to prune out as much as seventy to seventy-five per cent of the previous season's growth.

The Peach bears its fruit quite differently than any other type of tree, and this characteristic must be thoroughly understood. The fruit will appear on the twigs and branches which grew during the past summer. Although there will be blossoms the entire length of these twigs, the only flowers that should be allowed to set the fruit are those in the central one-third section of these twigs. Therefore, after the tree has been properly shaped by thinning, head back all of these twigs one-third of their length. Keep this in mind while doing the shaping.

The procedure to follow for the pruning of Peaches, is as follows:

First, cut out any dead branches which are on the tree. The older the tree the more of these there will be.

Second, cut out the least desirable of any crossing or rubbing branches. The branch that remains should be located as to contribute to the general good form of the tree. Also cut out any branches that bore fruit last summer. These will not bear fruit again, so remove them.

Third, the shape to be desired for the tree is that of a funnel, with the branches forming the sloping sides and the center top left open for complete penetration of sunlight. This open center will permit better ripening of the fruit.

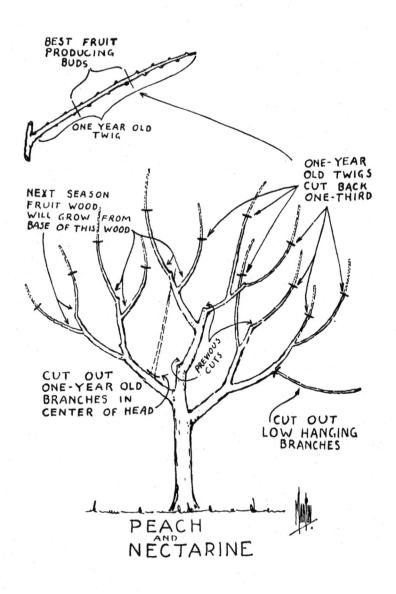

BEST FRUIT
PRODUCING
BUDS

ONE YEAR OLD
TWIG

ONE-YEAR
OLD TWIGS
CUT BACK
ONE-THIRD

NEXT SEASON
FRUIT WOOD
WILL GROW FROM
BASE OF THIS WOOD

CUT OUT
ONE-YEAR OLD
BRANCHES IN
CENTER OF HEAD

PREVIOUS
CUTS

CUT OUT
LOW HANGING
BRANCHES

PEACH
AND
NECTARINE

Fourth, begin to thin out the branches all through the tree, in such a way as to give an even distribution of branch growth throughout the entire tree. Always favor new branch growth. Do not hesitate to head back tall growth, because Peach wood is brittle, and a tall tree is almost sure to shed otherwise good limbs when they are heavy with fruit. Make the cuts carefully, with an eye to the location of the one year old twigs, or the fruiting branches. When finished, these one year old twigs should be about one foot apart all over the top of the tree.

In the case of trees that are more than ten years old, it may be necessary to select a new branch from the forks of the main branches to replace an old limb which has become diseased or broken.

Fifth, when the shaping has been completed, and at this point there should be better than sixty per cent of the tree on the ground, it is time to head back all of the one year old twigs and branches preparatory to fruit bud development.

As noted in a previous paragraph, cut back all of this one year old growth, one-third of its length. This heading back throws the maximum strength into the fruit buds which have been left.

A healthy Peach tree will set a very large amount of fruit, and about the first of June, the tree will voluntarily drop a proportion of the fruit that has already partially developed. If in your opinion, there is still too much fruit for the tree to support, the fruit may be hand thinned, but wait until the voluntary June drop has taken place.

There are other systems of pruning Peach trees, some of them involving the practice of summer pruning, but the above specified method is tried and true, and is by far the simplest for the average home owner to use.

65

PEAR

There are many varieties of Pears grown in various parts of the country, and although the habits of growth differ widely, the same system of pruning may be applied to them all. There is little similarity in growth between a dwarf variety and a Winter Nelis Pear, but the same principles apply, because they all produce their best fruit from fruit spurs, so the pruning to be done should favor these spurs.

Pruning is done during the winter months, while the tree is dormant.

Once again, the pruning system to be recommended is one that will apply best to the average backyard tree. There are a good many systems of pruning for orchard plantings, some of which would be practical for home use, but in order to eliminate confusion, the directions for just one method will be discussed here.

When the Pear tree is set out, the central stem should be headed, or cut off, at about thirty inches from the ground. If there are any lateral branches on the main stem, select three evenly spaced around the trunk, as well as up and down the main stem. See illustration on "Training Young Trees."

The first year should be devoted to training the scaffold limbs. It is more important to have a tree with a good sturdy foundation of limbs than to get one or two fruit a year early. Follow instructions of the "Training Young Trees" chapter.

The general habit of all Pear trees is to send up a great deal of tall whip-like branches from the center of the tree, especially in young trees, and the pruner must work every year to keep the head of the tree down, directing the vitality into the fruit bearing spurs, which will develop on the older wood.

66

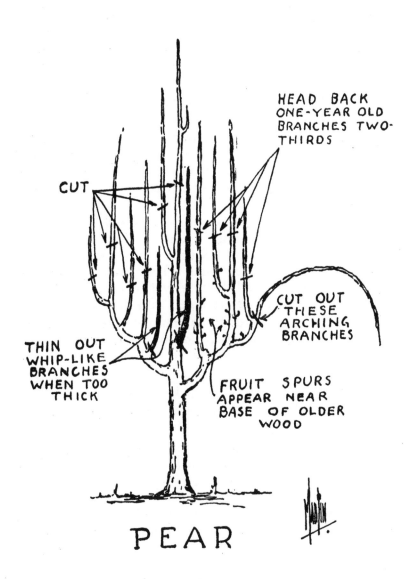

CUT

HEAD BACK
ONE-YEAR OLD
BRANCHES TWO-
THIRDS

CUT OUT
THESE
ARCHING
BRANCHES

THIN OUT
WHIP-LIKE
BRANCHES
WHEN TOO
THICK

FRUIT SPURS
APPEAR NEAR
BASE OF OLDER
WOOD

PEAR

67

The first thing to consider in the pruning of a Pear tree, is the removal of any dead wood, which on young trees will be very limited.

Second, cut out any interfering or crossing branches, that is, branches which are rubbing one another. Remove the one which contributes the least to the tree's good shape.

Third, thin out any new growths of whip-like tall shoots where they have grown in an overcrowded manner.

Fourth, head back the more substantial whip growths about two-thirds of their length. This cutting will force the tree's vitality into the main body of the tree-head, causing the greatest amount of strength to go to the fruit spurs.

Fruit spurs are the short stubby growths which have been developing on the older branches. They will vary in shape and length, but most frequently have a knob-like end, which is covered with new buds. These spurs will produce fruit year after year, and should never be pruned off unless they die from old age, or are killed with disease.

When the job of pruning is complete the head of the tree should be evenly spaced, allowing for an even penetration of sunlight. This is essential to the correct ripening of fruit.

Where the fruit production is kept in the lower portion of the tree head, there will be practically no need for any propping of limbs, due to heavy fruit production.

There is quite a tendency in some Pear varieties to produce a great deal of new growth towards the center of the tree, and where this habit shows up, the pruner should remove these central shoots, forcing the tree into a more spreading form. Otherwise your tree will soon become too tall for convenient picking, and the mass of central growth will cause the tree to become more of an easy prey to disease.

68

One of the worst diseases to attack Pear trees is a bacterial one known as "Pear Blight" or "Fire Blight," and is noticeable in the sudden dying of twig ends and leaves. As this disease travels within the stems and is spread by many causes, the diseased twigs should be cut off as soon as they are noticed. When cutting out this disease, always disinfect the shears after each cut with a strong germicide. Where the Blight gets into a main limb, it will be better to sacrifice the limb than to allow it to spread to the remainder of the tree. In cutting out any infected twigs, cut at least six to eight inches beyond where any infection shows up. All diseased twigs must be burned to destroy the harmful bacteria.

PECAN

The most important thing to be remembered in the growing of Pecan trees, is the training to proper shape during about the first five years of their growth. The natural tendency of the Pecan is for the outer branches to bend lower each year, due to the weight of foliage and fruit, so the initial training should be to develop a tree with the main framework branches as erect as possible. Some lateral branches may be encouraged to provide shade for the inner portion of the head.

Due to the natural habit of growth, a Pecan tree should be headed at about six feet from the ground. By this, it is meant not to allow any lateral branches on the trunk below six feet from the ground. The top will divide of its own accord higher up, so that it will not be necessary to stop the terminal growth of any upright branches, or the main central stem.

Any necessary pruning that is needed will consist of the removal of any interfering branches, and as the tree gets older, to remove the lower branches as they bend low enough to interfere with a person's walking beneath the tree. The Pecan is by nature a very tall growing tree, and as the nuts fall of their own accord when ripe, there is no necessity to try to alter the natural habit of growth, which is very beautiful in its natural proportions.

Pruning should be done during the winter months, while the tree is dormant and without leaves. Make any cuts smooth to the branch, without leaving a stub. This tree makes a satisfactory shade tree and will require a minimum of care.

PERSIMMON

The initial training of any variety of Persimmon is of utmost importance. Because of the brittleness of the branches, it is of great importance to develop a tree with a strong crotch and well spaced scaffold branches. See the instructions on "Training of Young Trees," for proper training procedure.

The necessary pruning for Persimmon trees is very simple indeed. The fruit is borne on current season wood, or in other words, a branch which grows this year will produce fruit this year, also fruit is borne on the one year old branches. So heading back will deprive the tree of its production of fruit.

Therefore, the only pruning which will be needed is to keep the tree well thinned out, and an even spacing of the fruit producing branches. Cut off any branches which have bent down low enough to interfere with working around the tree. These constantly lowering branches are always being replaced by cener growth on the inside of the tree.

In case a Persimmon tree becomes too tall, making it difficult to pick the fruit, the tall branches may be headed back severely. New shoots will spring out below where the limb was cut, and some of these may have to be thinned out during the summer if there appears to be too many.

The time for the annual pruning is during the winter months, while the tree is without leaves and the sap is dormant.

71

PLANTING YOUNG TREES

BALLED TREES, OR TREES IN CONTAINERS

Dig holes at least one foot larger in diameter than the diameter of the ball or container and one foot deeper than the depth of the ball or container.

In the bottom nine inches of the hole, fill in a mixture of one-half soil and one-half well rotted or composted manure. The market grade of steer manure will serve the purpose. Tamp or press this mixture down with the foot.

Fill in four inches of loose soil on top of the mixture. Tamp or press this firm.

Set the balled plant on top of the layer of soil, upright in the center of the hole. This should place the neck of the ball, or where it has been tied at the top, even with the general ground level. Do not remove sacking from ball, as this will soon rot. In the case of a canned plant, cut the can down two sides and bend the can away. Lift the ball of earth out, with the hands underneath, and set plant in center of hole.

Fill in loose soil around the ball. Build a basin for holding water by making a circular ridge around the diameter of the hole.

Allow water to run into the basin slowly, until filled.

By allowing the water to settle the loose dirt, instead of tamping the soil down, there will be no air pockets around the new roots to be developed.

Further irrigations as required by your particular soil.

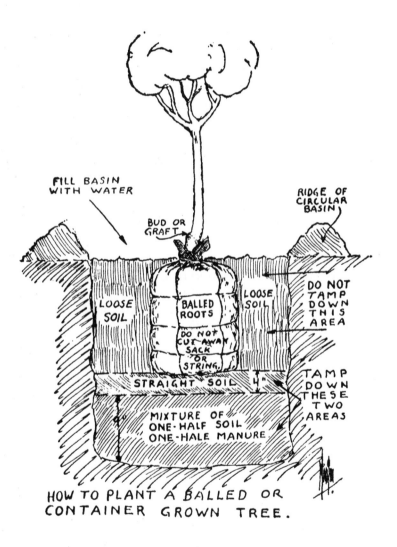

FILL BASIN
WITH WATER

RIDGE OF
CIRCULAR
BASIN

BUD OR
GRAFT

DO NOT
TAMP
DOWN
THIS
AREA

LOOSE
SOIL

BALLED
ROOTS

LOOSE
SOIL

DO NOT
CUT AWAY
SACK
OR
STRING.

STRAIGHT SOIL

TAMP
DOWN
THESE
TWO
AREAS

MIXTURE OF
ONE-HALF SOIL
ONE-HALF MANURE

HOW TO PLANT A BALLED OR
CONTAINER GROWN TREE.

BARE ROOT TREES

Dig hole at least one foot greater in diameter than the total spread of roots, when unwrapped and spread out, and one foot deeper than distance from where the soil surface was before on the trunk, and the lowest root.

Fill in lower nine inchs of hole with mixture of soil and well rotted or composted manure. Half soil, half manure. The market grade of steer manure will be suitable for this purpose. Press this mixture down firmly.

Fill in a layer of loose soil four inches deep, and tamp this down firmly.

Set tree in hole with stem in center, in upright position. See to it that roots are spread out as evenly as possible, then sprinkle soil onto roots, so that it will sift in around all of the fiber roots too. As soon as fiber roots are well covered, soil may be shoveled in and hole filled.

Where the tree is a grafted or budded variety, the graft should be left about two inches above ground level. In case of an unbudded seedling, the tree should be planted about two inches deeper than it was when grown by the nursery.

Make a basin for holding water by building a circular ridge around the diameter of the hole, and fill this basin with water slowly. The water will settle the soil around the roots more perfectly than the dry dirt can be tamped.

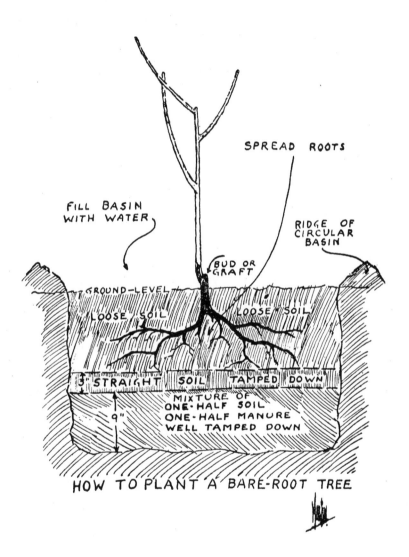

SPREAD ROOTS

FILL BASIN
WITH WATER

RIDGE OF
CIRCULAR
BASIN

BUD OR
GRAFT

GROUND-LEVEL

LOOSE SOIL   LOOSE SOIL

3" STRAIGHT SOIL TAMPED DOWN

MIXTURE OF
ONE-HALF SOIL
9"   ONE-HALF MANURE
WELL TAMPED DOWN

HOW TO PLANT A BARE-ROOT TREE

75

GENERAL PLANTING INFORMATION

Don't mix fertilizer of any kind with soil to go next to roots of a newly planted tree or shrub, whether balled, bare-root, or container grown.

Keep the soil around the roots of fruit trees at as even a moisture content as possible. Irrigate as often as necessary, according to your soil.

A mulch of straw, or even dead weeds, around the basin under a tree, will help to preserve the moisture and prevent the surface from baking.

Always cultivate to the same depth. This keeps the feeder roots at one depth, and they will not be damaged by too deep a cultivation.

Never spray fruit trees while they are in full bloom, as this will ruin the flower pollination and no fruit will set on.

The feeder roots of any plant are usually found in a circle around the skirt or eves of its top. Remember this when watering and fertilizing. The roots between the feeders and the trunk have ceased to take in either food or moisture, and are merely useful as anchors and conduits of the vital tree processes.

In the average soil, one surface inch of water will penetrate to about one foot of depth, furnishing adequate moisture. Two inches of water to a two foot depth, etc. Keep the moisture content of your soil as near constant as possible.

Any soil requires a constant addition of organic matter, as well as fertility, to keep it from baking hard, and to keep alive the essential soil organisms.

76

PLUMS AND PRUNES

These two fruits are the same with the exception that the Prunes have a greater sugar content, and therefore will dry without removing the pit. One system of pruning will apply to both types, because they all have the same fruiting habits. Prune the trees in the winter while the trees are dormant.

The Plums and Prunes do their best fruit producing from fruit spurs, which may appear on any branch after it is two or more years old. Therefore the pruning system should be one which will develop these fruit spurs.

For the training of a young Prune or Plum tree, follow the directions as specified in the chapter on "Training Young Trees."

Because of the nature of these two types of fruits, it is of utmost importance to develop a very strong and well balanced framework of branches. The general shape of the most desirable type of tree to be grown, is that of a funnel, or inverted pyramid, with the center well filled with fruit producing limbs.

Until the tree is about ten years old, the training program will continue, by heading back the long whip-like branches about two-thirds to three-quarters of their length, where they have grown in a position to benefit the desired form for the tree. Any new branches that do not benefit the shape of the tree should be cut out entirely. Branches should be spaced not closer than one foot from each other, to allow for easy picking and light penetration.

After about the third year, the fruit spurs will begin to develop on the oldest branches, and these small gnarled, stubby growths will produce fruit year after year. Always save the branches with fruit spurs, wherever possible.

When the tree is ten years old or more, the new growth

77

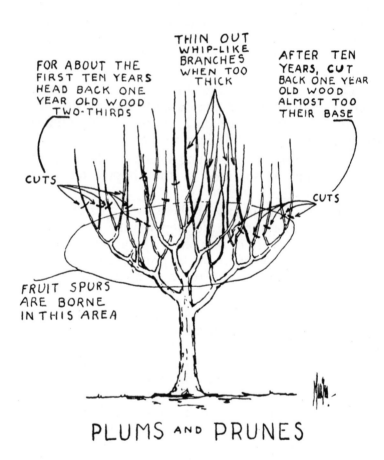

FOR ABOUT THE FIRST TEN YEARS HEAD BACK ONE YEAR OLD WOOD TWO-THIRDS

THIN OUT WHIP-LIKE BRANCHES WHEN TOO THICK

AFTER TEN YEARS, CUT BACK ONE YEAR OLD WOOD ALMOST TOO THEIR BASE

CUTS

CUTS

FRUIT SPURS ARE BORNE IN THIS AREA

PLUMS AND PRUNES

78

must be cut out almost entirely every winter, leaving it only where it is necessary to refill a space where an old limb has been taken out. As the outer branches gradually lower with the weight of fruit and foliage, they should be cut out during the winter. This removal of a main limb should be balanced by leaving an equal amount of new wood on the inside of the tree to take its place.

The procedure for pruning Plum and Prune trees, ten years old and older, would be as follows:

First, cut out any dead wood and crossing or interfering branches.

Second, remove any old limbs that have lowered their position to the extent of being in the way.

Third, start in removing new growth by cutting out the least desirable branches first. Cut these out smooth to the branch from which they grew, leaving no stub.

When there is nothing left in new growth but those which are evenly spaced throughout the tree, head these back to about one-third to one-quarter of their length. The older the tree, the more they should be headed back.

Pruning of these trees should be done from a ladder as much as possible, because any climbing on the tree itself will destroy a great many of the fruit spurs.

POMEGRANATE

The pruning of this variety of fruit is very simple in method, but rather difficult from a standpoint of labor, due to the toughness of the wood and close habit of growing.

Natural tendency of the Pomegranate is to develop a mass of erect growing shoots or branches, which if one allows them all to stay will grow into a plant to which very little can be done.

For the first three or four years try to encourage as spreading a plant as possible, by cutting out the shoots that spring from the lower inside of the plant. As the plant develops, allow no new shoots to grow that appear within two feet of the ground. Pull them off as they start. A single trunk bush will be much easier to care for in the future. Where young plants are set out, this type of training will be easy.

Pomegranates will produce fruit from any wood after it is one year old, but the quality and size of the fruit will be better if the top is kept well thinned out, allowing plenty of sunlight penetration.

The natural tendency for the Pomegranate is to grow into an erect arching shape, with the outer branches constantly lowering. Therefore, it will be necessary to cut out this outside growth from time to time, as the necessity arises, wherever a branch is too low, and in the way.

Pruning should be done during the dormant period of winter.

OLIVE

Because this book does not cover commercial production pruning, the treatment of the Olive will be given more as an ornamental tree as they are most generally used in our gardens today. The fruit production is purely secondary, if not usually ignored.

The Olive, as an ornamental fruit tree, may be trained in various ways or allowed to grow naturally. Because of its versatility it adapts itself to many conditions with a minimum of care. Pruning as applied to an Ornamental Olive tree cannot affect the fruit production in any way.

Olives are usually planted because of their delightfully informal habit of growth and any pruning will be governed entirely by the likes or dislikes of the owner, as to whether a headed tree or bush type is wanted. The Olive will naturally take on a very gnarled method of growing, and when this effect is desired, do not even remove interfering branches, or those which are rubbing against one another. The Olive is practically disease resistant, so that these branches which are rubbing one another will not be detrimental to the tree.

The only thing which will be essential in the pruning of an Olive is the removal of dead wood as it appears. This work may be done at any time of the year, whenever a dead branch is noticed. Any cuts that are made should be cut very close, leaving a smooth wound with no stub. A cut of this sort will heal over rapidly.

The Olive will stand almost anything in regard to pruning, so any cutting that is to be done will be dictated entirely by the individual requirements of the tree in one's own yard.

ORANGE

Citrus fruits in general require very little in the way of pruning and the Orange, regardless of whether it is Navel, Valencia, or other varieties, is no exception. These fruits have a habit of growth which virtually train themselves for the first four to seven years, leaving very little for the owner to attend except to irrigate and fertilize properly.

As with all citrus trees, the Orange develops a head with very close set leaves, excluding practically all sunlight from the inside of the tree. This condition causes minor die-back of small twigs on the inside of the tree, which should be cut out at least twice each year. There is no particular time of season most suited for this work, as it may be done at any time. When this minor cutting is to be done, it will be better to work your way into the inside of the tree head rather than try to reach in from the outside.

While doing this die-back cutting, watch out for any crossing or interfering branches which may be rubbing against each other. Cut out the interfering branch which contributes the least to the general good shape of the tree.

Any pruning cuts that are necessary should be made close to the branch without leaving a stub, from which decay may travel into the limb.

As the Orange tree grows older the outer branches will bend lower toward the ground, and as they droop to less than two feet from the ground, the ends should be removed to prevent fungus disease from spreading from the soil to the fruit on the lower branches. This pruning should be done as soon as the fruit has been picked from these lowering branches.

Remove any shoots or suckers that may appear on the trunk of the tree. If these are removed when they are only an inch or two in length they may be rubbed off by a downward movement of the hand against the tree trunk.

Orange branches are sufficiently tough to withstand a considerable load of fruit without breaking, and even though an overload of fruit may distort the position of a branch, do not put a prop under a heavily laden limb to help support the fruit, because this action will cause a very rapid weakening of the limb itself. Props are to be avoided except as a very last resort.

In the case of a very healthy tree, there will frequently be long sucker-like shoots which appear and grow from the center of the tree. These should be pulled out when they are about one foot long. Pulling is a better method than cutting, because when the sucker is pulled, practically all of the latent buds to be found around the base of the sucker will be pulled away with it, and it is impossible to cut close enough to remove them.

QUINCE

This fruit may be grown in two different forms, either as a tree, with single trunk, or as a bush. Because of the nature of the plant, the latter system will be the easier. The same system of pruning will apply to both methods of shaping the tree.

The manner in which the Quince bears its fruit determines the system of pruning. The best fruit buds will be found as lateral or side buds in the upper half of the one year old twigs. These same branches will produce good fruit for about three or four years, so that a system of thinning out the oldest branches is all that will be needed in the way of pruning.

Pruning of the Quince will not become necessary until the fourth winter that the tree is put out, and then should be done every winter thereafter. Keep the top evenly spaced with upright shoots or branches, cutting out the ones which have arched over to the ground from the weight of fruit.

Do not head the branches back as this will take off all the fruiting possibilities of the plant. If the plant has become too tall, thin out the tallest branches well down into the base of the plant.

RASPBERRY

The pruning instructions for raspberries, as with other of the bramble fruits, are very simple. The point to remember is that the best berries will be borne on canes which have grown one full season. In other words, canes that started from the root, and grew this summer, will produce berries next summer, and when these canes have produced their summer crop they should be removed.

Pruning is done during the winter months while the plants are dormant.

Cut off at ground level, all canes which produced fruit last season. This will leave an ample supply of young canes which have grown for one complete growing season, and which will produce fruit during the coming summer.

All raspberries have a tendency to spread out over more area, as a result of increased root development, and so as the plants grow, it will become necessary to spade up some of these spreading roots in order to keep the original row or hill. These roots which have been dug up may be used for planting new areas.

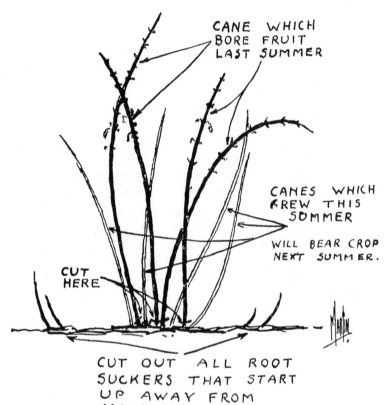

CANE WHICH
BORE FRUIT
LAST SUMMER

CANES WHICH
GREW THIS
SUMMER

WILL BEAR CROP
NEXT SUMMER.

CUT
HERE

CUT OUT ALL ROOT
SUCKERS THAT START
UP AWAY FROM
MAIN HILL OR ROW.

RASPBERRY

TRAINING YOUNG TREES

The success of any fruit tree, particularly the deciduous types, depends a great deal upon the initial training which it receives during the first three years after being planted out. The instructions will apply to any type of deciduous tree with exceptions of Walnuts and Pecans, so they will be given according to what should be done in each successive year.

First Year. Let it be assumed that the fruit tree has been purchased from the nursery and is already planted in the ground according to the "Planting Instructions" as given earlier in this book.

Cut off the main leader or central stem, at about thirty inches from the ground. If there are any lateral branches on the tree, make this cut immediately above a good strong lateral branch at about the height mentioned above.

Then select two other lateral branches, if other than a whip growth, one about eight inches below the top one, and another about sixteen inches below the top. Make your selection of these branches so that when you look straight down above the center, the three branches trisect about equally, an imaginary circle drawn around the stem. See illustration.

Next, head these three lateral branches back to about one-half their total length. These three branches are the framwork of the future tree, and by selecting them spaced in the above manner, the tree will develop a crotch that is less apt to split in later years.

As the tree grows allow only two buds to develop branches on each of the framework branches; one at the end, and one about halfway between the end and the base. Let these branches grow to the full development without

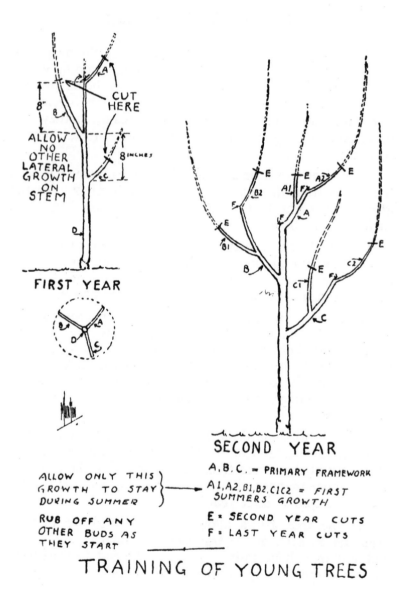

FIRST YEAR

8"
ALLOW NO OTHER LATERAL GROWTH ON STEM
CUT HERE
8 INCHES

SECOND YEAR

ALLOW ONLY THIS GROWTH TO STAY DURING SUMMER

RUB OFF ANY OTHER BUDS AS THEY START

A.B.C. = PRIMARY FRAMEWORK
A1, A2, B1, B2, C1C2 = FIRST SUMMERS GROWTH
E = SECOND YEAR CUTS
F = LAST YEAR CUTS

TRAINING OF YOUNG TREES

further summer pruning, and rub off any shoots that may appear on the trunk as suckers.

Second Year. There should now be six well developed branches on the young tree. Cut back these branches about two-thirds of their length. Cut just above a strong bud or lateral branch. Head back the lateral branches one-half their length.

The tree is now ready to produce fruit, and the system of pruning that is recommended for the particular variety should be carried out.

All of this pruning should be done during the winter while tree is dormant, except where summer cutting is specified.

WALNUT

This variety requires little pruning, providing the initial training has been done properly. The young tree first set out should be topped, or cut off, at about eight feet from the ground, and no lateral growth allowed to develop below six feet. All three framework branches to develop as specified in "Training of Young Trees" chapter. Except that there should be about 24 inches between top and lower branches instead of 16.

The tendency for Walnut trees is for the outer branches to constantly lower each year, with the weight of fruit and foliage. As these branches get low enough to interfere with cultivating, etc., they can be cut off during the winter months while the sap is inactive. Be sure that the sap is dormant by making a trial cut on a live twig, and watch it for a few minutes to see if there is excessive bleeding. If bleeding occurs make no further cuts until the sap is dormant.

To counteract the tendency of the constantly lowering outer branches, new branches should be encouraged in the center of the tree. These, as time goes on, will gradually work their way outward.

The top of the tree should be kept free of any interfering or rubbing branches, as well as all dead wood. Do this at the dormant period, during the winter.

EXCERPTS FROM H. H. THOMAS'S
PRUNING MADE EASY

Edited by Christine Schultz

A GENERAL SURVEY

Knowledge of pruning is essential for the successful cultivation of fruit trees. Understanding the most effective methods is crucial, but luckily, they are easy to learn. To optimize the output of an orchard or garden, the grower must consider the characteristics of different tree varieties, in addition to those of the individual tree. Fruit trees tend to be pruned too severely, and they would bear heavier crops if they were pruned less. Another common fault occurs when one plants too many fruit trees in a limited area. After few years, they will take up more room than the planter had anticipated, and each year they will become increasingly crowded. Having bought the trees and tended them for a number of years, the planter is disinclined to do away with any of them, and the only other way of making room for them is to cut back the branches hard. This results in a luxuriant growth of leaves and branches at the cost of the fruit.

Fruit trees must have ample room for proper development. The branches must be fully exposed to air and light, otherwise a successful harvest is impossible. Also, soil type and positioning are important things to consider in the pruning process.

WHY FRUIT TREES FAIL

If planted in rich soil, young fruit trees will grow vigorously, but they will not bear fruit for a number of years. Further, the more their branches are pruned, the more freely they will grow. As a result, planters often renounce fruit cultivation owing to their disappointment year after year of scanty crops. Although fruit trees need deeply cultivated soil, they should not be heavily manured; old mortar or lime rubble is excellent material to mix with the soil for all fruit trees, and especially for stone fruits (e.g. Cherry and Plum).

A MATTER OF IMPORTANCE

It is also important to keep the uppermost roots within three or four inches of the surface of the soil when planting. Deep planting is not conducive to fertility. As a result, planters can avoid severe pruning, which rarely pays in fruit cultivation, by better preparing the ground and giving the trees sufficient room for their development. The first instruction, therefore, in pruning trees is a negative one—prune them as little as possible. In fact, you should prune your trees just enough to keep them within the allotted space and prevent overcrowding of the shoots and branches. More abundant crops will be the reward.

PRUNING NEWLY PLANTED FRUIT TREES

A newly planted tree is one that has been put in the ground between October and March, and its pruning is attended to in the spring months after planting. Thus it may have been in the ground for six months or only for one month. In dealing with the pruning of such trees, two methods are in general practice, and planters must decide which one to follow.

One method advises planters to prune the trees in the first spring; the other approach is to postpone pruning until a year later. The latter recommendation, however, has been shown to be less effective, and the beginner may be advised to disregard it and to prune his trees during the spring months (March or early April) following planting.

It is a safe rule to severely prune newly planted fruit trees. Unless the branches are cut back fairly hard, they are unlikely to start into growth except at the top, and the lower parts may remain bare, thus giving rise to an ill-balanced and unshapely tree.

You may now wonder: By how much should the trees be shortened? Which branches should be cut? Let us first address the last question. It is important that the amateur realizes that he must only cut the branches that grew during the past summer. He must not, except in special circumstances, interfere with older branches. They should be shortened to anywhere from one half to one third in size. In other words, they should be left half as long or two thirds as long as they were. If the branches are weak, cut them back so that only one third remains. If they are moderately vigorous, let them be shortened by one half. If they are really strong and thick, and the trees were planted in autumn, they may need to be shortened by only one third. It is, however, safer to prune severely.

If the trees have been in the ground only a month or two, the branches should not to be left more than half as long as they were. Trees planted late in the spring are slow in starting into growth, and their progress the first season may be poor. It certainly will be a poor harvest if they are pruned lightly, but if pruned severely, the chances are that the buds toward the base will be forced into growth and will produce good branches.

During the first few years, the goal is to build up a shapely tree furnished with the requisite number of branches. If the foundation is well laid, fruit production will follow as a matter of course. If, however, the tree is pruned lightly in its first year, the chances of the tree having a satisfactory life are jeopardized. Thin, weakly branches cannot bear a heavy crop of fruit.

Therefore at this first pruning, do not trouble over crop output just yet. Prune hard for the purpose of securing good strong branches to provide a firm foundation on which the tree can be built upon. In later years, the pruning can be modified according to the needs of the grower, the kind of tree, and the variety of fruit.

Thin, weakly shoots should be cut right out for they will block up the center of the tree and crowd the main branches. If there are side shoots on the lower parts of the branches that have been shortened, they should be pruned within two buds of the main branches. Those who advocate deferring the pruning of newly planted fruit trees until twelve months or more after planting argue that by that time, young trees will have become established and will respond better to severe pruning. Unless care is taken to keep the roots moist in dry weather, this method may be particularly advisable for fruit trees grown on poor land where growth is slow. However, generally it is better to prune in March or April immediately following planting.

PRUNING STANDARD FRUIT TREES

Apple, Pear, Plum, Cherry, and Damson are the fruits commonly grown as standards. Though the ways of pruning established trees differ to some extent, standards may conveniently be considered together since their general treatment is similar. The initial pruning of newly planted standards is important, for it exercises a considerable influence on the form and solidity of the tree. The foundation of the branches must be firmly laid; unless the limbs are strong, the tree will scarcely be able to bear the weight of a heavy crop, which results in disfigured and broken limbs. Therefore, the pruning of the newly planted standard must be severe.

All thin and weakly shoots should be cut right out, and the main branches shortened to within about eighteen inches of the base of the past summer's growth. Then the buds will start growing strongly, and the tree will have a firm foundation of branches. For the first few years, it will be necessary to regulate the development of the branches by shortening the leading shoots (those at the ends of the branches) by about half in the winter. This is achieved by cutting out all weak growths and shortening the side shoots on the main branches in the summer and winter (see Martin's chapter on pruning Apple trees). In later years when the trees are of a fair size and well established, the chief aim is to keep the main branches well apart and to cut right out any weakly or otherwise useless shoots; if left, they will cause overcrowding and will effectually put an end to fruitfulness.

Thinning out—not cutting back—is the most important detail in the pruning of standard fruit trees. If the branches are about eighteen inches apart from each other, fruit buds will develop naturally along them in due course, and there will be little cutting back to be done either in the summer or winter. It will, of course, be necessary to look over the trees both in July and in January for the purpose of shortening the side shoots, but if the above directions are observed this work will not be arduous.

The failure of standard trees is generally due to over-crowding. Unless the branches have the full benefit of sunlight and air, the fruit buds will not develop, the trees will continue to grow freely, and ultimately they will be crowded with thin, useless shoots that are unable to bear fruit and prevent stronger branches from doing so.

Planters often ask what can be done with standard trees that have reached this state. They are full of weak, spindling shoots that never bear fruit, and they have been so neglected that they have developed into a thicket of growth. The first thing is to cut the inside shoots right out. Then the number of branches must be limited—as previously stated they should be about eighteen inches apart. Old and worn-out fruit spurs should be shortened, or cut out if they are crowded, and side shoots that have been allowed to grow unchecked should be cut back to within two or three buds of the main branches on which they developed.

PRUNING CORDON TREES

The fruits most commonly grown in the form of cordons are Apples and Pears. The Plum is occasionally grown in this form, but it is not very satisfactory, and amateurs who wish to grow Plums are advised to purchase pyramid or standard trees. A cordon tree is one that is restricted to one stem, or two or three stems; it has no branches other than the annually shortened side shoots, which eventually become "spurs," on which blossom buds and fruits are borne. It is obvious that trees of this kind must be pruned severely, otherwise they soon branch out, lose their characteristic shape, and cease to be cordons.

So far as their actual pruning is concerned, there is little to be said beyond that it must proceed on the conventional lines, referred to in preceding section dealing with Pruning Standard Fruit Trees. The leading shoot, that which extends the stem, should be allowed to develop naturally in the summer, but in the winter, it is shortened by one half or one third, according to whether it is rather weakly or vigorous. In July or August, the side shoots are shortened to within about six buds of the base of the current summer's growth (not counting the small leaves at the bottom), and in the winter, they are further cut back within two buds or so.

This is certainly rule-of-thumb pruning, but it is the only thing one can do if the shape of the tree is to be preserved. It does not suit all varieties of course, and when choosing Apple trees to be grown as cordons, it is wise to avoid those of vigorous or otherwise unsuitable growth, such as Newton Wonder, Bramley's Seedling, Lane's Prince Albert, and Norfolk Beauty.

Over the course of years, the original stem may become weakly, and as a result, the spurs will lose vigor and will not blossom satisfactorily. This matter can be remedied by training another stem to take the place of the original one, so that you can eventually cut out the latter altogether. The process is a gradual one, and takes several years to accomplish.

When this course is deemed necessary, a promising shoot as low down in the tree as possible should be taken care of and allowed to grow unchecked during the summer months. At the winter pruning, it is cut back to within fifteen inches of the base. Every year it should be allowed to progress to that extent; thus in the course of three years, it will be nearly four feet high. Then the work of getting rid of the old stem may begin. This should gradually be shortened as the new stem makes progress, until over the course of time it is cut away altogether and the new stem takes its place. By adopting this method, cordon Apple trees can be kept in a healthy and fruitful state for an indefinite period.

PRUNING TRAINED FRUIT TREES

Trained fruit trees are those grown against a wall or on a special support in the open garden. They are of various shapes, chief of which include single, double-stemmed, treble-stemmed, and gridiron or four-stemmed cordons, along with fan-shaped and horizontal cordons. Peach, Nectarine, and Apricot are commonly grown only as fan-shaped trees, but Apple, Pear, Plum, and Cherry are grown in both forms, though the latter is generally trained as a fan-shaped tree.

When the trees are young, it is necessary to prune and train them carefully to obtain tiers of branches at a uniform distance from each other on the horizontal espaliers and to preserve the fan shape of the tree. Amateurs would do well to obtain trees three or four years old and not to attempt to train them from "maidens."

In pruning horizontal espaliers, the side shoots must be "stopped" or cut off at about the sixth leaf in the summer and shortened again in the winter, and the shoots at the ends of the branches—the leading shoots, as they are called—are shortened by about half in the winter.

In the following spring, care must be taken to select a shoot that can be trained as nearly as possible in a straight line with the older part of each branch, so that the latter continues to grow in exactly the same direction. Disbudding, or the removal of superfluous shoots, is an important part of the work of pruning trained fruit trees because it saves much cutting of the branches later on and helps prevent unnecessary branch pruning. Side shoots must, however, be pruned in the summer and winter in order to preserve the symmetry of the tree.

PRUNE TOP OF TREE FIRST

In the summer, it is wise to prune the upper part of the tree before the lower part and to restrict the sub-lateral, or secondary shoots, to one leaf because the tendency of the tree is to grow more strongly at the top than at the bottom. By allowing the shoots on the lower branches more freedom, a more uniform growth will be obtained.

It is difficult to keep fan-shaped Peach and Nectarine trees in good condition unless great care is taken to preserve young shoots as near the base as possible. This will allow them to be tied in to replace the older branches when, after the fruits have been gathered, these are cut out. In fact, it is not an easy matter to keep trained fruit trees of any kind in a healthy and fruitful condition unless they are given frequent attention and skilled care. The trees soon become ill-balanced unless the vigorous shoots are restricted and the weaker ones encouraged by allowing them more freedom of growth.

Above all, it is essential to prevent the vigorous growth of the top of the tree as it will weaken the lower branches. The latter are likely to die, thus spoiling the form, which is difficult to restore when the tree is no longer young.

SUMMER PRUNING

The pruning practiced during the summer months is of real importance in the cultivation of fruit trees. If it is neglected, satisfactory results are unlikely. This process consists of shortening those shoots that are not required to extend the branches, to thus prevent overcrowding and expose the buds on the lower parts of the shoots—those of chief importance—to sunlight and air. When fruit trees are cultivated in a restricted area, pruning is essential to prevent the shoots and branches from becoming crowded and to direct the development of the trees in the ways desired.

If summer pruning is not practiced, a good deal of the growth that formed during the summer months will have to be cut away in the winter since there will be no room for it. It is to the advantage of the trees that they are prevented from making these superfluous shoots. This is the view taken by the professional gardener, and summer pruning has been an established practice in gardens for generations.

It is a matter of importance to prune at the right time. It cannot be said that one period is suitable for all fruit trees. Those grown against sunny walls and fences are much more advanced in growth by early July than others in the open garden; obviously, therefore, they need attention earlier in the summer than the latter. Such trees ought to be pruned during the first fortnight in July—the exact time depends on the condition of the shoots. When these are seven or eight inches long, they ought to be pruned. It is usually found best to summer prune fruit trees in the open garden towards the end of July and beginning of August.

PRUNING THE SIDE SHOOTS

This form of pruning consists of shortening (by cutting or pinching off with finger and thumb) the shoots of the current summer's growth other than those at the ends of the branches. It is the usual practice to leave these unpruned until winter. Most gardeners recommend leaving six leaves on each of the summer side shoots—the small leaves at the extreme base not being included. If the shoots are cut down much lower than this, there is a possibility that the buds at the base will start into growth, and we do not want that to happen until the following spring.

PRUNING SUB-LATERALS

A few weeks after the shoots have been pruned or "stopped," the buds in the axils of the uppermost leaves will start to grow, and the shoots they produce are known as sub-laterals. They are of no permanent value, because they will be cut off during the winter pruning; therefore, they must be "stopped" when one or two leaves have developed. If summer pruning is practiced earlier than at the times recommended, the sub-laterals grow vigorously, and a good deal of labor is caused in pruning them.

ROOT PRUNING

One always hesitates to recommend the root pruning of fruit trees because it seems such an unnatural sort of thing to do. Yet if a fruit tree persists in making vigorous unfruitful shoots, which become still more abundant the more severely they are pruned, and the room available for the development of the tree is limited, root pruning seems the only practicable thing to do. I doubt if it is of much use so far as old-established trees are concerned; however, it is of far greater value in dealing with young trees.

The object of root pruning is to prevent the trees from becoming filled with gross, unfruitful branches, and it is a far better practice than first allowing them to make vigorous growth and then taking them up and cutting back the roots severely.

The kind of root pruning chiefly recommended is not concerned with cutting back old, thick roots, but with shortening those of recently planted trees. Most young fruit trees are likely to grow vigorously during the first few years after they are planted, and it should be the purpose of the grower to prevent their doing so. It is not difficult to do this, providing the essential details are attended to regularly during the first three or four years. All that is necessary is to take up the trees (a matter that is very easily done when they have been in the soil only for a year) shorten the thickest of the roots by half or so, and replant, taking care to cover the uppermost roots with only about three inches of soil. This kind of root pruning is a simple matter, and it is undoubtedly the best.

Sometimes it is thought necessary to root-prune large fruit trees that have been established for some years, yet do not bear fruits. But it is not likely to be of much avail unless the branches are kept well apart from each other and all superfluous shoots are cut out. I have known old trees to be severely root-pruned and to suffer such a check to growth that they were almost killed; for two or three years, they scarcely made any growth, and bore no fruits. Root pruning certainly did not pay, for if the old trees had been uprooted and young ones planted to replace them these would have proved far more profitable over time.

In dealing with large established trees, it is a mistake to root-prune all the roots on one occasion. Those on one side of the tree ought to be pruned one year and those on the opposite side the following year. The way to proceed is to dig a trench two feet or so wide and of such a depth that it will be possible to get well underneath the roots. The soil must be forked away from the latter and placed outside the trench until all the thick, strong roots are exposed. Pay particular care to search for those roots directly underneath that grow straight downwards. When found, they must be shortened to two or three feet. In replacing the soil, take care to lay the roots in as nearly a horizontal direction as possible and to firmly pack the soil around them. The best time to carry out root pruning is late in October when most of the leaves have fallen from the branches.

NOTES

NOTES

NOTES

NOTES

NOTES

NOTES

Lightning Source UK Ltd.
Milton Keynes UK
UKHW020610170220
358846UK00009B/280